THIS

AWESOME

SKETCHBOOK BELONGS TO

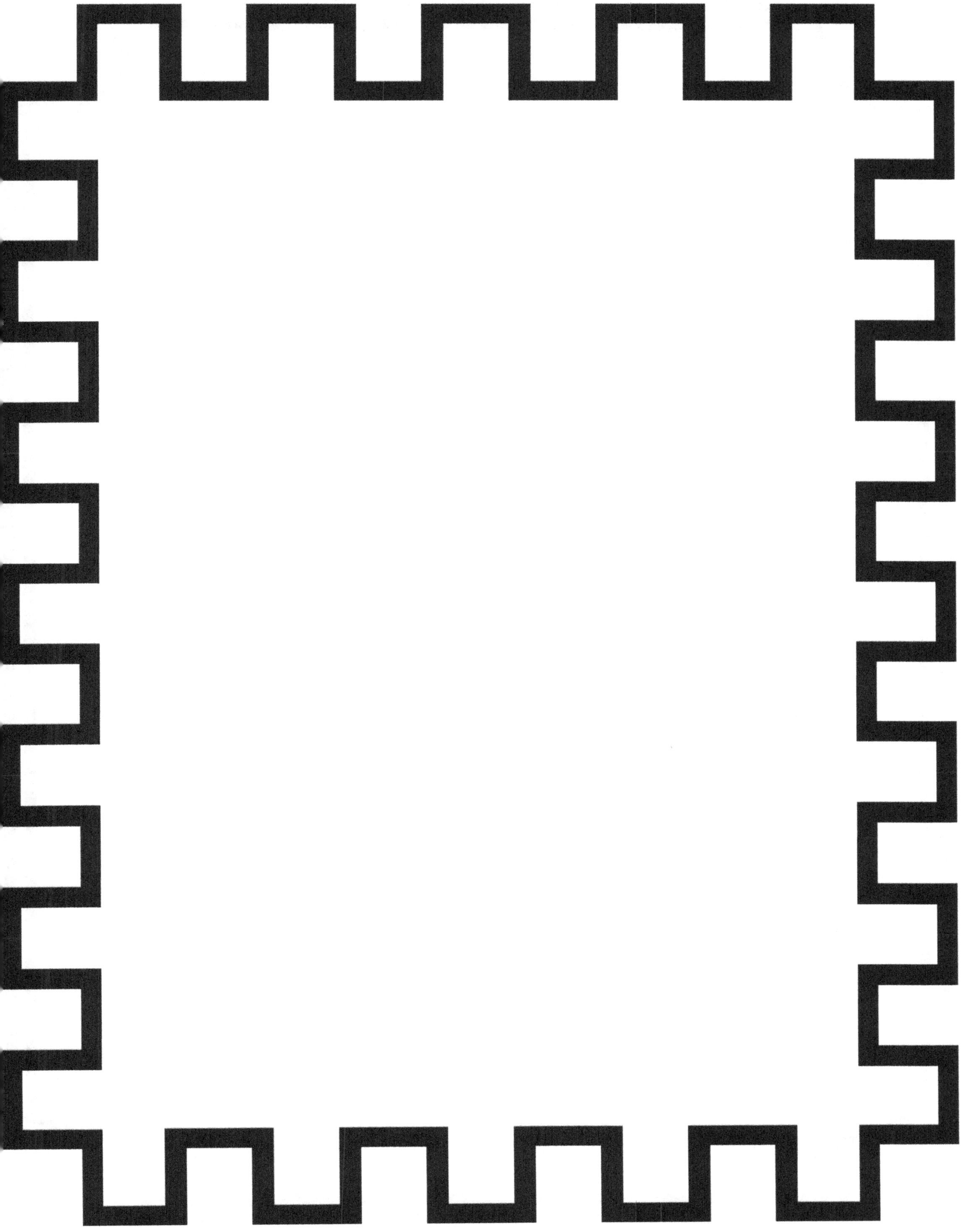

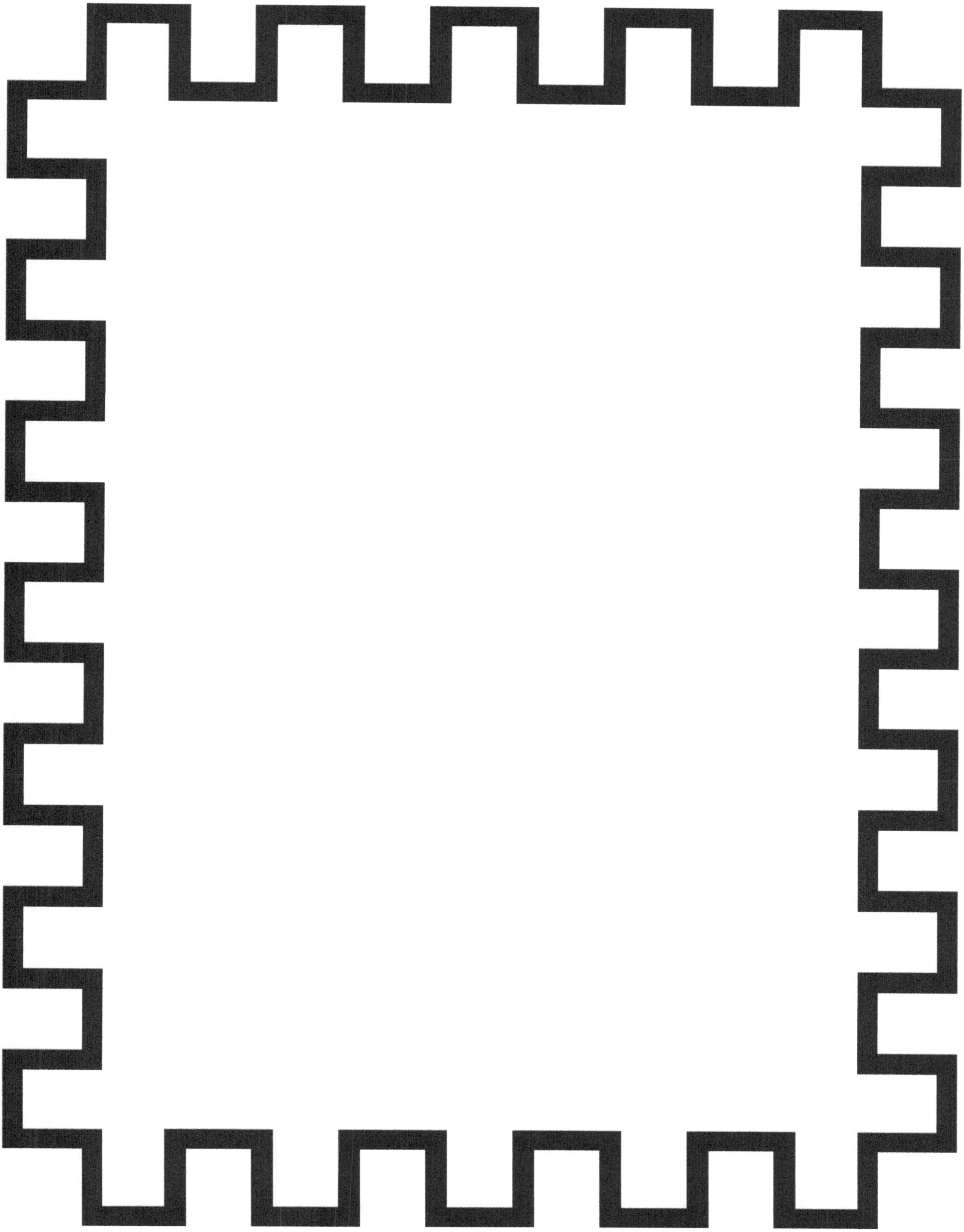

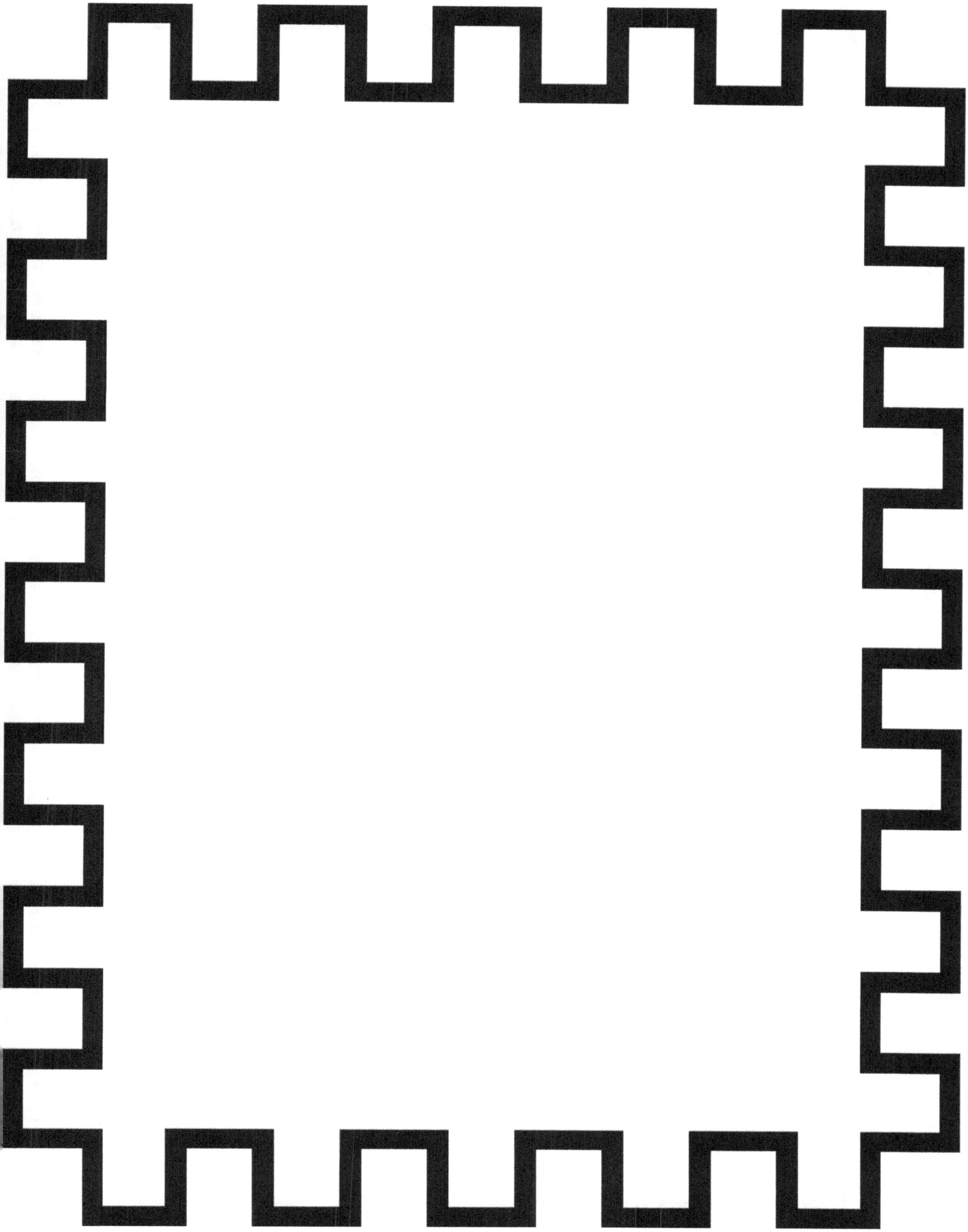

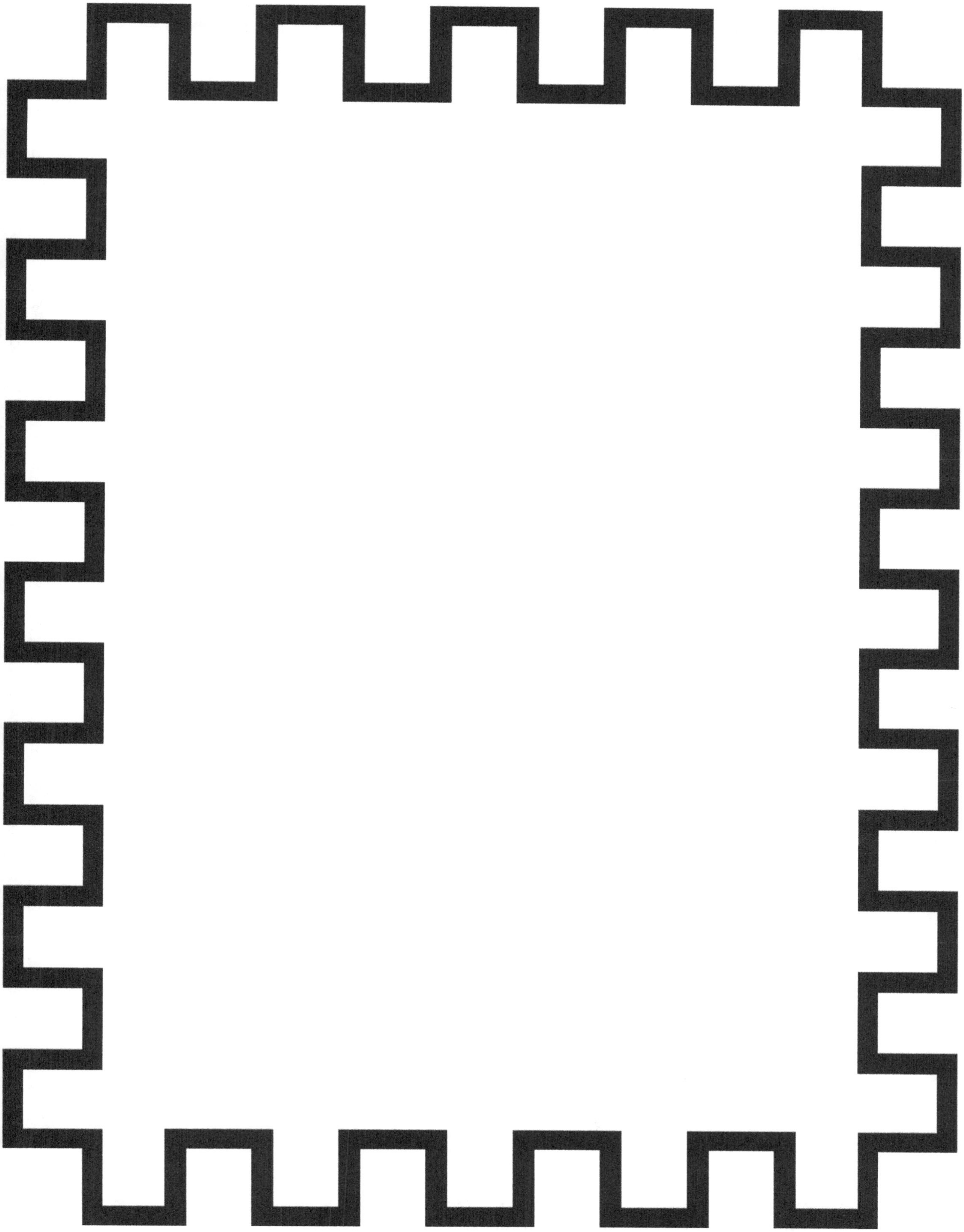

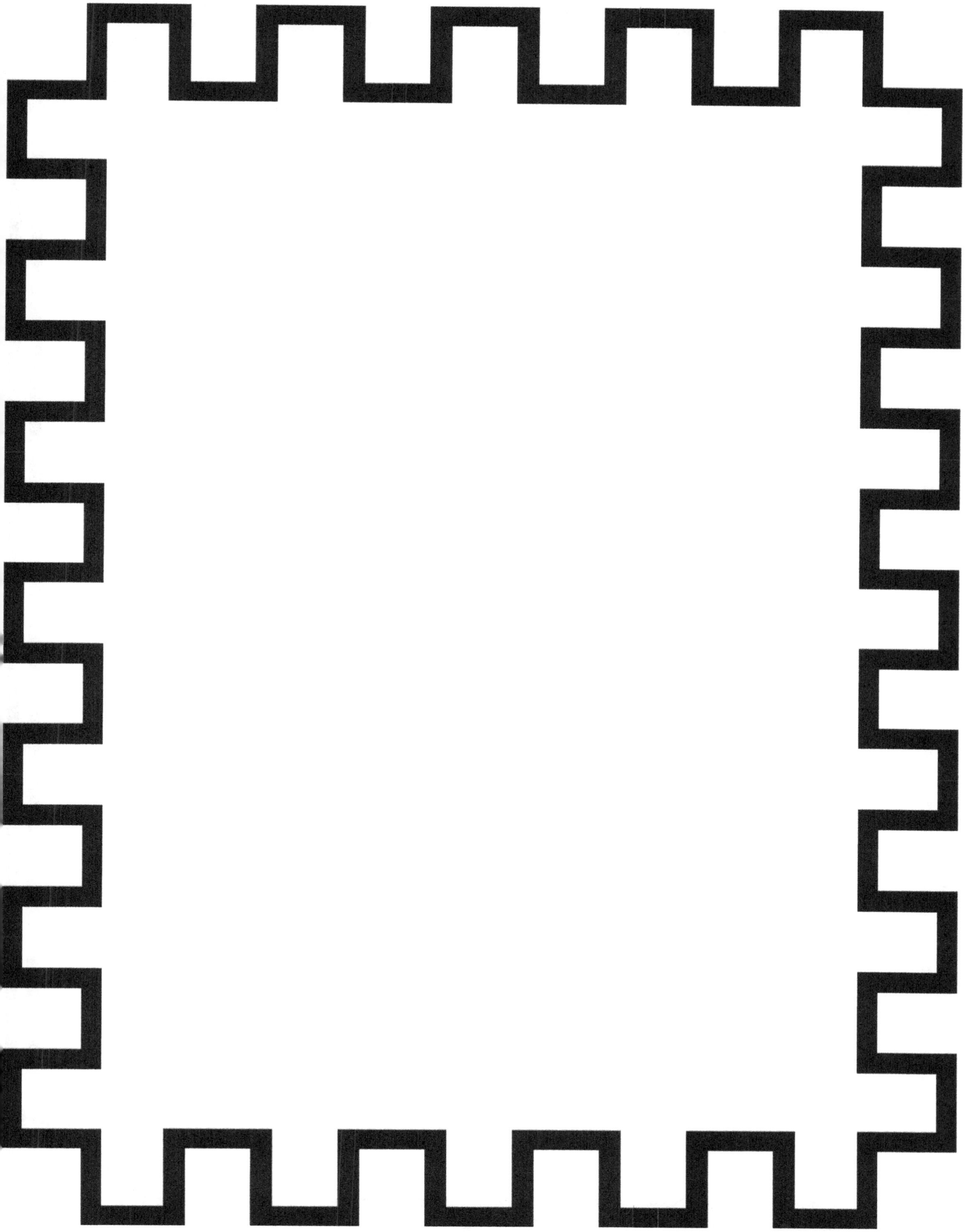

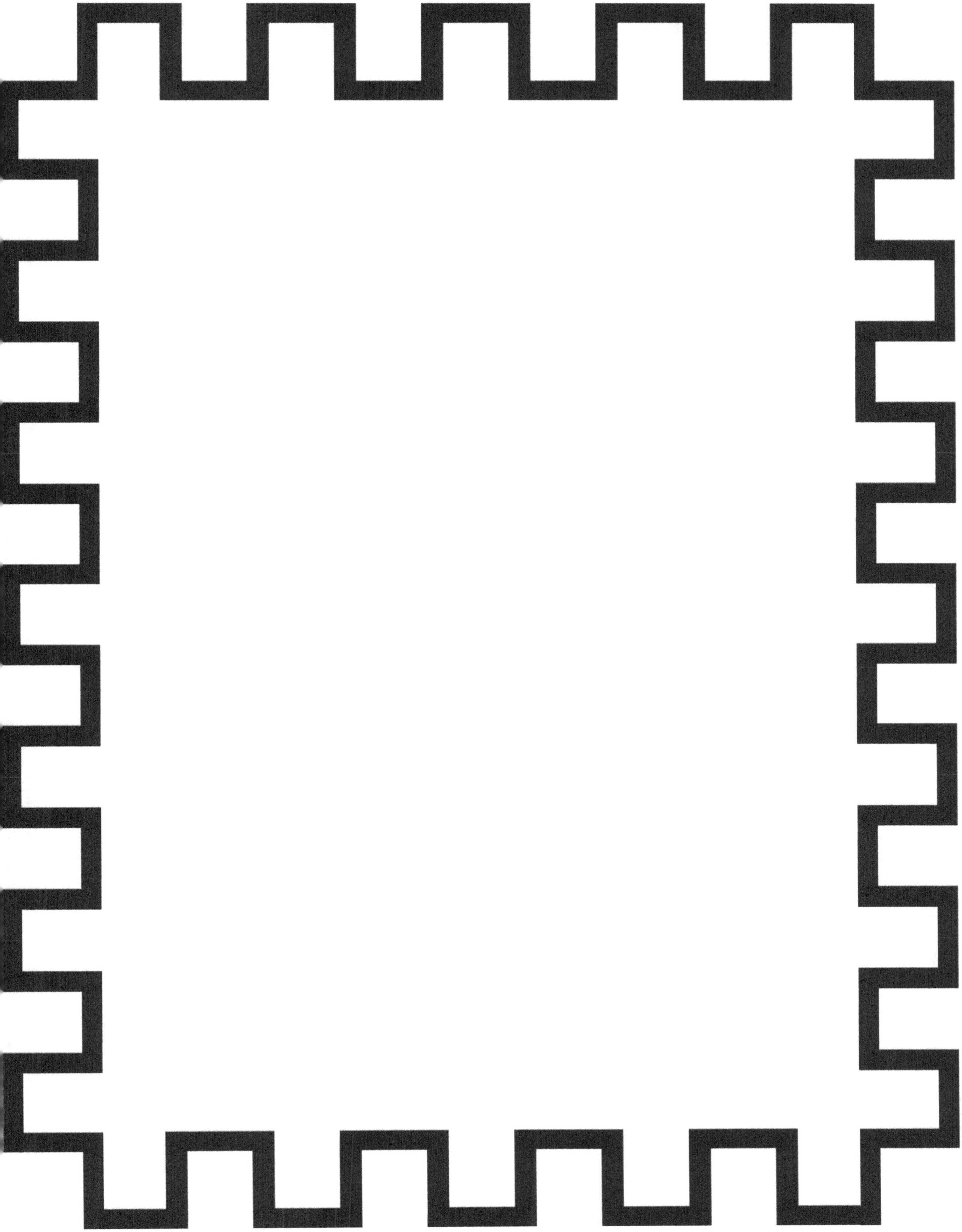

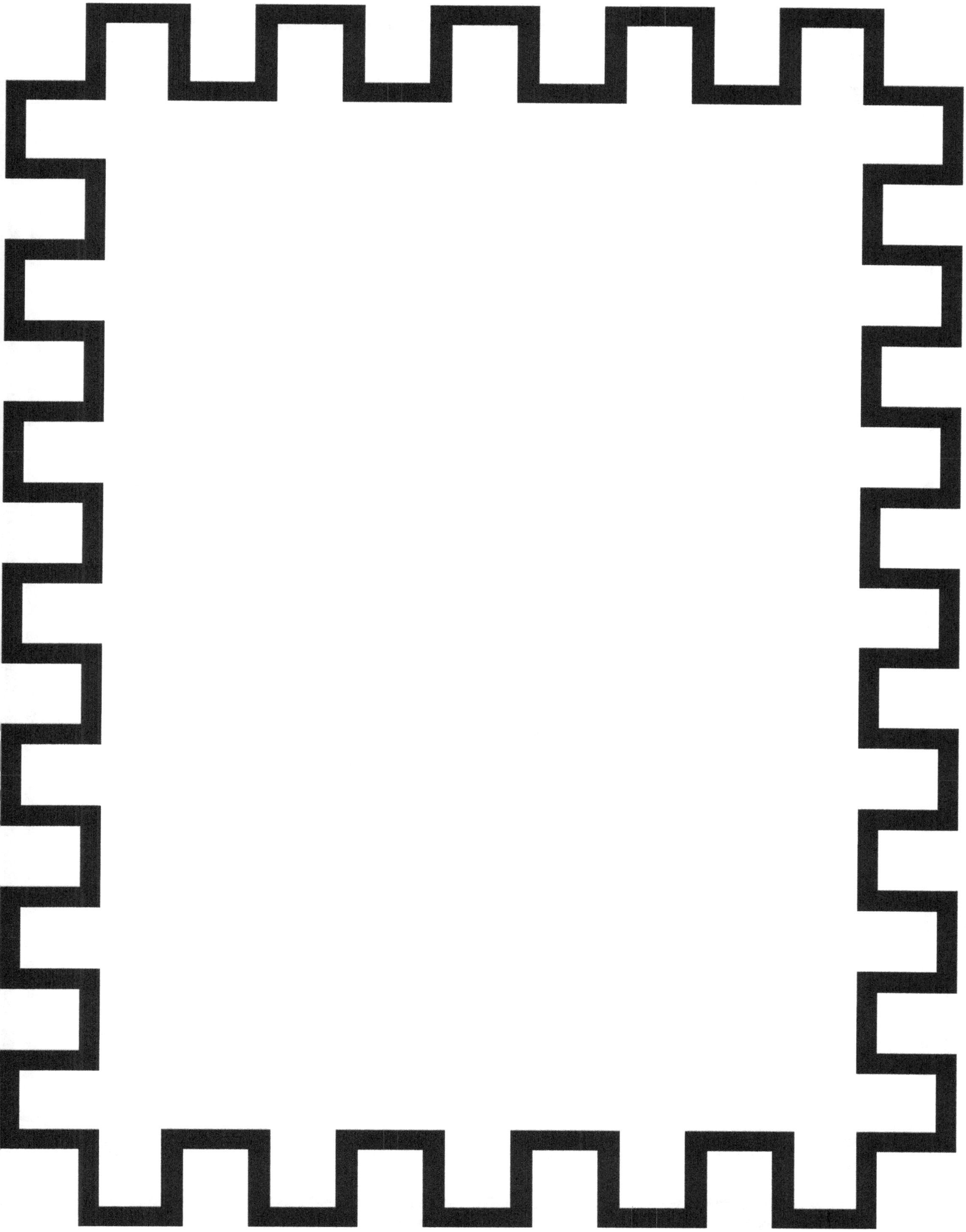

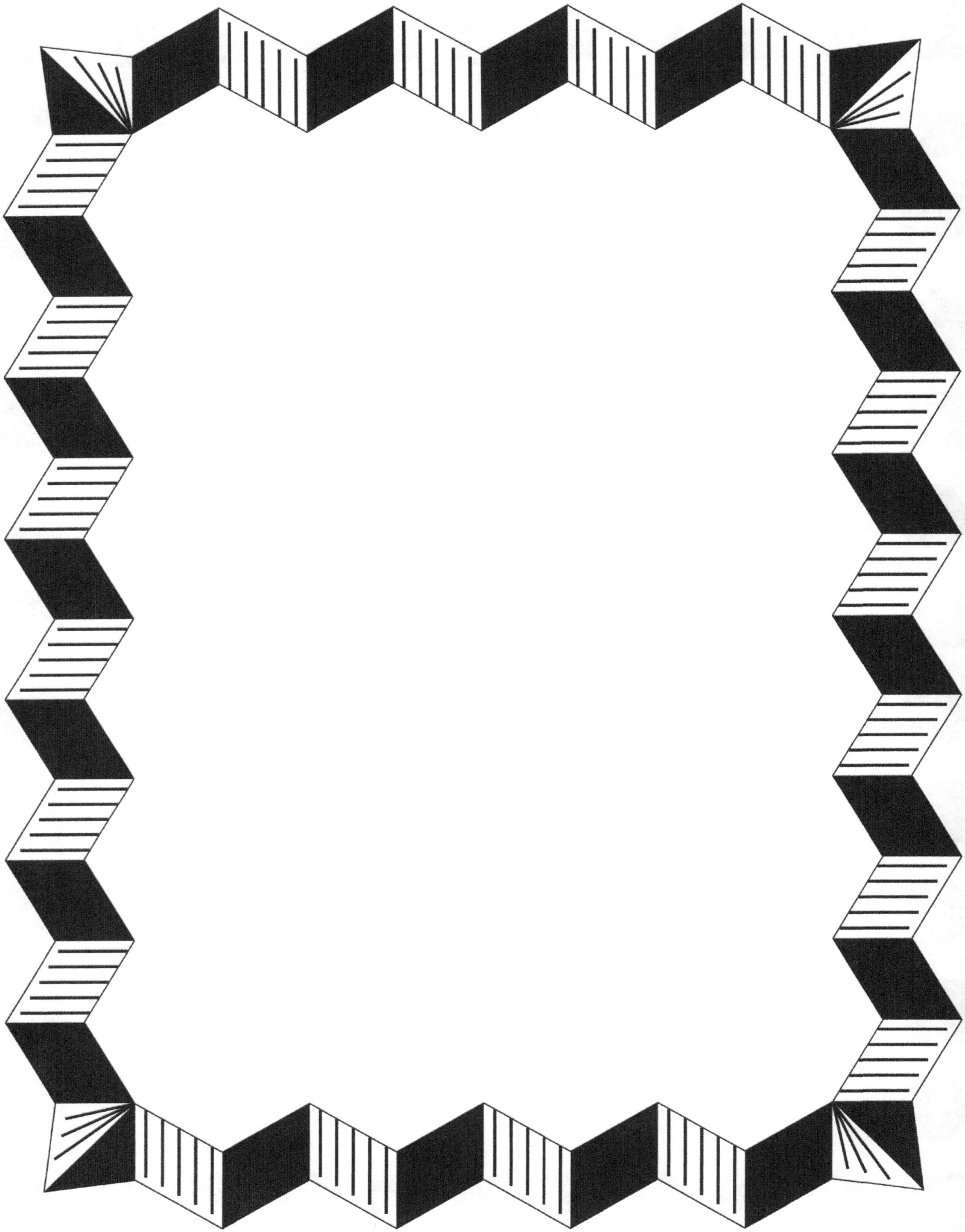

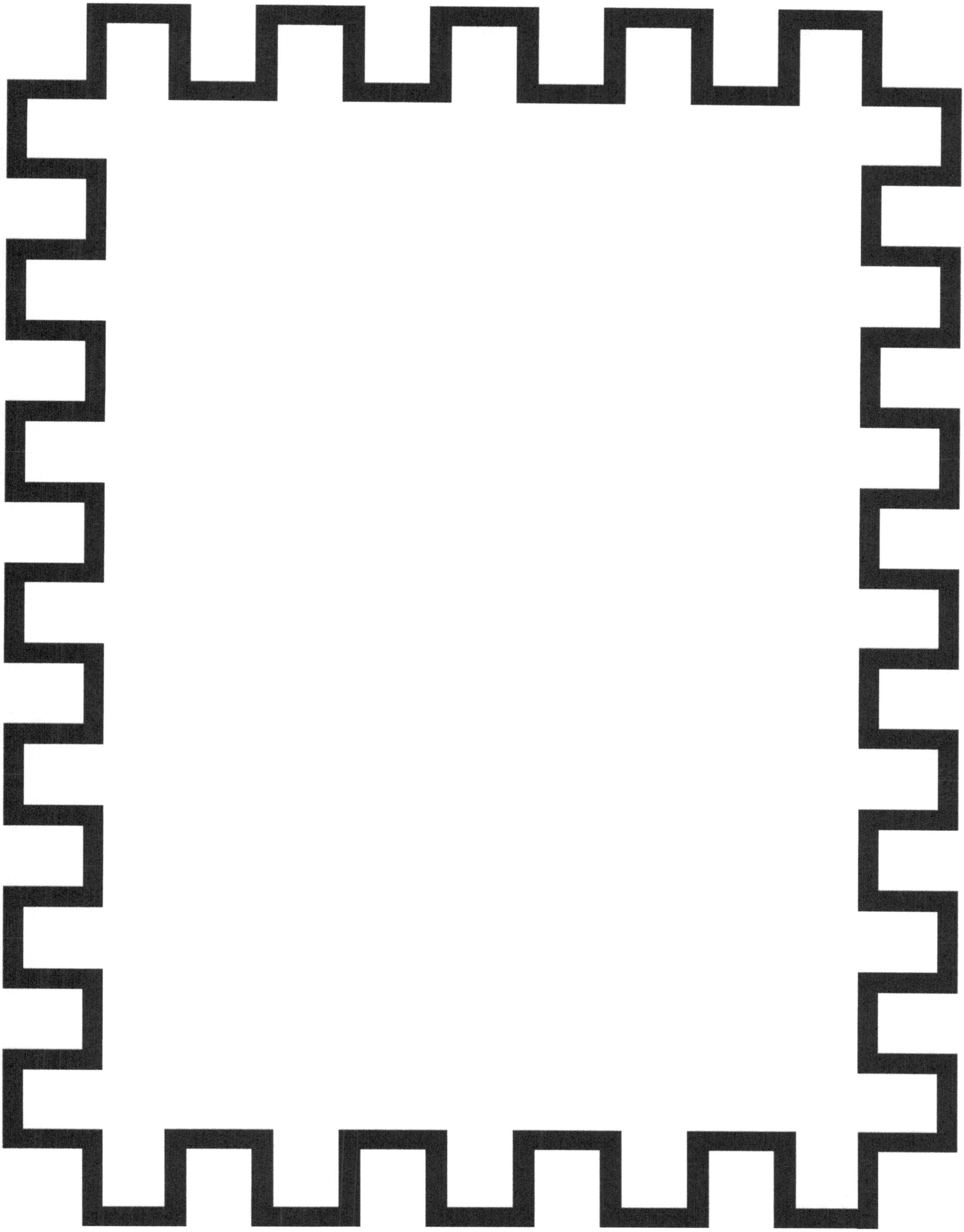

Made in the USA
Monee, IL
10 March 2023

29582537R10063